ASANA USER GUIDE

The Complete Handbook to Use this Platform for Task
Management, Project Planning, Team Collaboration and
Goal Tracking

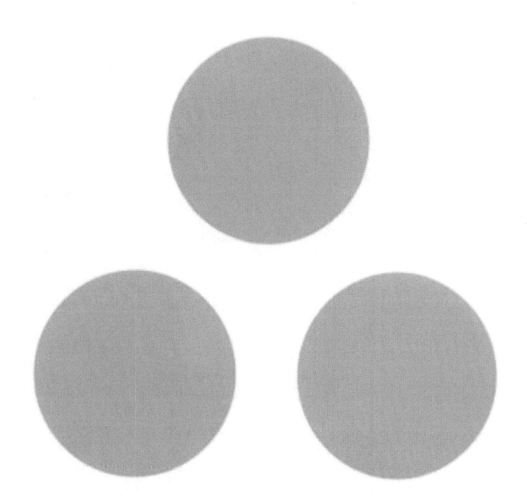

BURT P. SOUZA

DISCLAIMER

The contents of this book are provided for informational and entertainment purposes only. The author and publisher make no representations or warranties with respect to the accuracy, applicability, completeness, or suitability of the contents of this book for any purpose.

The information contained within this book is based on the author's personal experiences, research, and opinions, and it is not intended to substitute for professional advice. Readers are encouraged to consult appropriate professionals in the field regarding their individual situations and circumstances.

The author and publisher shall not be liable for any loss, injury, or damage allegedly arising from any information or suggestions contained within this book. Any reliance you place on such information is strictly at your own risk.

Furthermore, the inclusion of any third-party resources, websites, or references does not imply endorsement or responsibility for the content or services provided by these entities.

Readers are encouraged to use their own discretion and judgment in applying any information or recommendations contained within this book to their own lives and situations.

Thank you for reading and understanding this disclaimer.

TABLE OF CONTENTS

CHAPTER ONE
INTRODUCTION TO ASANA

<u>What is Asana?</u>

Asana, Inc. was established by Dustin Moskovitz and Justin Rosenstein in 2008, is a San Francisco-based American software company. Its core product, Asana, is a web and mobile application designed to assist teams in organizing, tracking, and managing their work. The service became commercially available in April 2012, and by September 2020, the company's valuation had reached $5.5 billion following its direct listing.

As a software-as-a-service platform, Asana enhances team collaboration and work management by enabling users to create projects, assign tasks, set deadlines, and communicate within the platform. It also offers reporting tools, file attachments, calendars, and goal-tracking features.

In 2022, Asana added new organizational tools, such as My Goals, Automatic Progress Updates, and integrations with Google Workspace and Figma. The company had previously released its API in April 2012, allowing third-party developers to interact with the platform through a RESTful interface for data input, updates, and automated processes.

In April 2021, Asana launched Asana Partners, facilitating cross-platform integration with its project management software.

Subsequently, in July 2021, Asana introduced an app for Zoom, making it accessible within the video-conferencing software. By 2023, Asana expanded its product capabilities to include generative artificial intelligence features.

Features of Asana for Project Management

Explore the dynamic range of Asana's features across all tiers with this comprehensive list:

What sets Asana apart

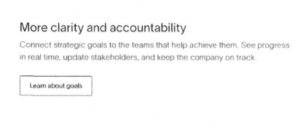

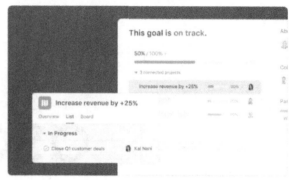

Work, Project, and Task Management:

- Asana AI: Enhances planning clarity and accountability, speeds up workflows, and scales work efficiently.

- Projects: Organize work into shared projects using lists or kanban boards for initiatives, meetings, and programs.

- Tasks: Define who is responsible for each task and its deadlines.

- Subtasks: Break down tasks into smaller steps or additional parts.

- Task Assignees: Clearly designate task ownership.

- Sections and Columns: Organize tasks into sections (list view) or columns (board view) to align with workflow stages.

- Custom Fields: Create various custom fields (single-select, multi-select, number, text) in projects and portfolios to capture and track information, receive updates, and sort/filter like a spreadsheet.

- Forms: Capture work request details directly connected to projects for centralized tracking.

- Due Dates and Times: Set deadlines and specific times for tasks to ensure timely completion.

- Start Dates: Indicate when work should begin to meet deadlines.

- Timeline: Use a Gantt-style view for better planning and scheduling.

- Attachments: Add files from your computer or cloud storage (Google Drive, OneDrive, Dropbox, Box) to tasks or messages.

- Likes: Use likes to acknowledge tasks, comments, or give approvals.

- Multi-home Tasks: Include the same task in multiple projects without duplication.

- Dependencies: Clarify which tasks are ready to start and which are dependent on others.

- Rules: Automate manual processes such as task triaging, assignment, and field updates.

- Templates: Start projects quickly with templates and save custom templates for recurring use.

- Approvals: Request and provide approvals directly within Asana.

Communication:

- Task Comments: Comment on tasks to clarify requirements, and @mention teammates or other work items.

- Proofing: Leave comments on images or PDFs that turn into tasks for easy tracking.

- Project Messages: Discuss project progress to maintain momentum.

- Team Pages: View all team projects and share all-team messages and announcements.

- Languages: Available in multiple languages, including English, Chinese, Russian, Dutch, and more.

- Rich Text: Use rich text in larger fields to organize thoughts with numbered/bulleted lists.

Views:

- My Tasks: Plan your day with a prioritized to-do list.

- Inbox: Filter notifications for projects, messages, and tasks you follow.

- List View: Create, filter, and format tasks in a grid-like structure.

- Search: Quickly find work without extensive organization.

- Saved Searches: Save specific search criteria for repeated use.

- Workload: Manage team bandwidth and make informed staffing decisions.

- Calendars: View tasks on a calendar to see due dates.

- Files View: Quickly find project files in a gallery view of attachments.

- Colorblind Friendly Mode: Access the full Asana color palette in colorblind friendly mode.

Reporting:

- Goals: Set, track, and manage company goals while connecting work to its purpose.

- Milestones: Use task milestones as key markers of progress.

- Portfolios: Monitor strategic initiatives and project statuses in one place.

- Status Updates: Quickly craft status updates to share with stakeholders.

- Dashboard: Use real-time custom charts to identify blocked or off-track work and export charts as needed.

Team Management:

- Teams: Organize projects and connect teammates with shared calendars and messages. Control team privacy settings.

- Collaborators: Add teammates as collaborators to follow task progress and receive updates.

- Guests: Collaborate with external partners for free.

- Permissions: Limit project access, create private or public teams and projects.

- Admin Controls: Assign super admins and admins to manage members, enforce password complexity, and use SAML and Admin API for additional controls.

- Privacy Controls: Limit access to projects, create private teams for sensitive work, or make teams public.

- Data Security: Export or delete data easily, with backups on a separate server.

Integrations:

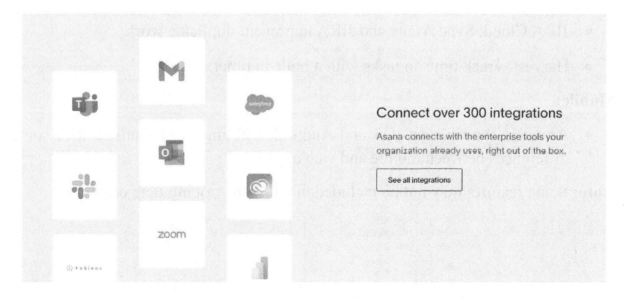

Connect over 300 integrations

Asana connects with the enterprise tools your organization already uses, right out of the box.

See all integrations

File Creation and Sharing:

- Dropbox, Google Drive, Box: Attach files directly to tasks using a built-in file picker.

- Adobe Creative Cloud: Integrate with Creative Cloud tools to share designs and incorporate feedback without leaving the app.

Communication:

- Slack: Create, complete, and edit tasks directly from Slack. Automatically post updates to Slack channels.

- Asana for Gmail and Outlook: Turn emails into actionable tasks tracked in Asana.

- Zoom: Create or link to Zoom meetings from tasks, with transcripts and recordings attached after the meeting.

Other Top Integrations:

- Google: Connect with Google Drive, log in with Google SSO or SAML, and add tasks from Chrome.

- Microsoft: Integrate with Teams, Office 365, Outlook, OneDrive, and Power BI.

- Salesforce: Track follow-up work and create projects automatically at key stages.

- JIRA Cloud: Sync Asana and JIRA to prevent duplicate work.

- Harvest: Track time on tasks with a built-in timer.

Mobile:

- Asana is available on iOS and Android, offering most features with some differences between mobile and web apps.

Note: Some features may not be included in all Asana pricing tiers or plans.

The world's top companies trust Asana

See all case studies →

Overstock

Overstock manages hundreds of partner relationships with Asana.

Hubspot

Increased production of advertising campaigns for clients by 50% each month.

Figma

Figma's product team reduced meeting time by 50% with Asana.

Zoom

Zoom saves 133 work weeks per year with Asana.

<u>Benefits of Asana for Project Management</u>
Benefits:

Improved Organization:

- A centralized platform consolidates all project-related information and communication.
- Simplifies the tracking of tasks, deadlines, and project progress.

Enhanced Collaboration:

- Streamlined communication minimizes misunderstandings and promotes teamwork.
- Real-time updates keep everyone aligned and informed.

Increased Productivity:

- Clear task assignment and responsibility boost accountability and efficiency.
- Automating routine tasks saves time for more strategic activities.

Better Decision Making:

- Real-time data and analytics enable informed decision-making.
- Custom reports offer insights into team performance and project health.

12

Scalability:

- Suitable for teams of all sizes, from small startups to large enterprises.

- Flexible features adapt to the evolving needs of any organization.

Integration and Customization:

- Seamlessly integrates with existing tools and workflows to enhance productivity.

- Customizable features and API allow for tailored solutions to specific business requirements.

Asana's comprehensive features and benefits make it a versatile and powerful tool for effective project management, ensuring teams can work more efficiently and achieve their goals.

Who Should Use Asana?

Asana is a flexible tool that serves a diverse array of users and organizations. Here are some of the key groups that can greatly benefit from using Asana:

Teams and Departments:

- Project Management Teams: Perfect for overseeing projects from initiation to completion, including planning, execution, and tracking.

- Marketing Teams: Excellent for organizing campaigns, creating content, and monitoring marketing efforts.

- Product Development Teams: Ideal for managing product roadmaps, tracking features, and facilitating collaboration between designers, developers, and other stakeholders.

- Sales Teams: Useful for managing sales pipelines, tracking leads, and coordinating with marketing and customer support.

Companies and Organizations:

- Startups: Provides essential structure and organization for growing teams, aiding in efficient scaling.

- Small and Medium-sized Enterprises (SMEs): Equips teams with tools to handle various projects without needing a large budget.

- Large Enterprises: Supports complex workflows and integrations, making it well-suited for large organizations with diverse requirements.

Professionals and Individuals:

- Freelancers: Helps organize tasks, manage client projects, and track deadlines.

- Remote Workers: Enhances communication and collaboration for remote and distributed teams.

- Consultants: Assists in managing client engagements, tracking deliverables, and maintaining clear communication.

Industries:

- Technology: Supports software development, IT projects, and tech startups.

- Creative Agencies: Manages creative projects, client work, and collaboration among designers and writers.

- Education: Assists educators and administrators in managing school projects, academic research, and classroom activities.

- Nonprofits: Organizes fundraising campaigns, volunteer coordination, and program management.

Use Cases:

- Event Planning: Coordinates event logistics, task assignments, and deadlines.

- Product Launches: Manages timelines, marketing activities, and cross-functional collaboration.

- Content Production: Tracks content creation, editorial calendars, and publication schedules.

- Client Management: Centralizes client projects, communication, and deliverables.

Asana is adaptable to the needs of various users, making it an excellent choice for improving organization, collaboration, and project management across different contexts.

CHAPTER TWO
GETTING STARTED WITH ASANA

Setting Up Your Asana Account

Asana provides a streamlined and collaborative project management solution. Here's a step-by-step guide to setting up your Asana account and getting started:

Sign Up and Log In:

- Visit Asana's website and click "Get Started."

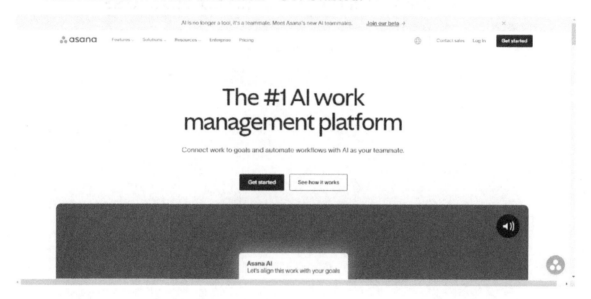

- Choose to sign up with your email and create a password or use your existing Google account (for paid subscriptions).

- Verify your email address if you sign up using email by completing setting up your account.

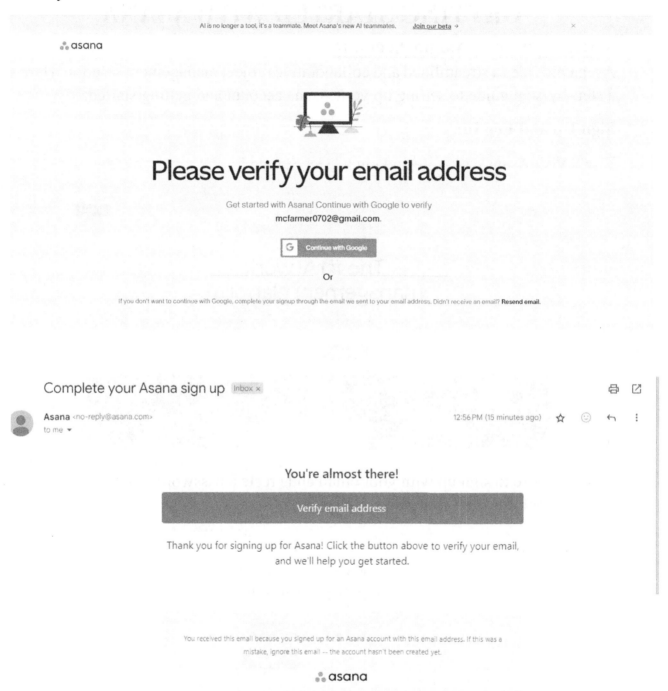

Welcome to Asana:

- Explore the introductory screens that showcase Asana's functionalities.

Create Your Workspace (Optional):

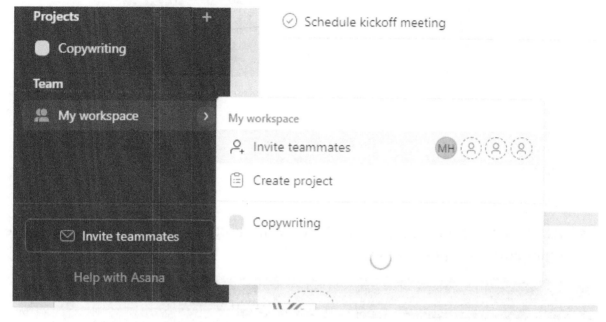

- Asana allows you to create workspaces for different purposes (e.g., work team, personal projects).

- Choose a descriptive name for your workspace. You can invite teammates by their email addresses if applicable.

Familiarize Yourself with the Interface:

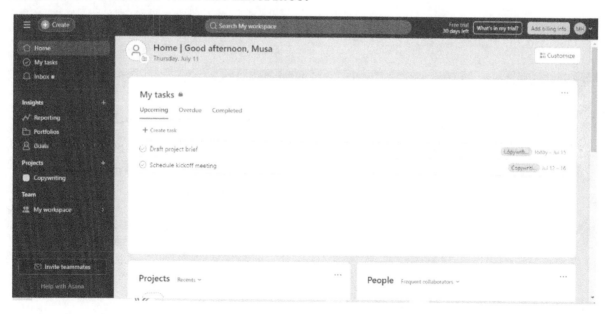

Personalize Your Profile (Optional):

- Click on your profile picture or name in the top right corner.

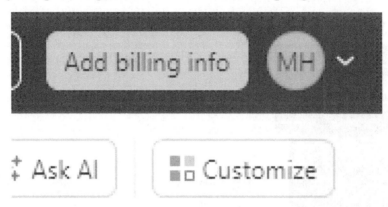

- Access profile settings to add a photo, set notification preferences, and explore other customization options.

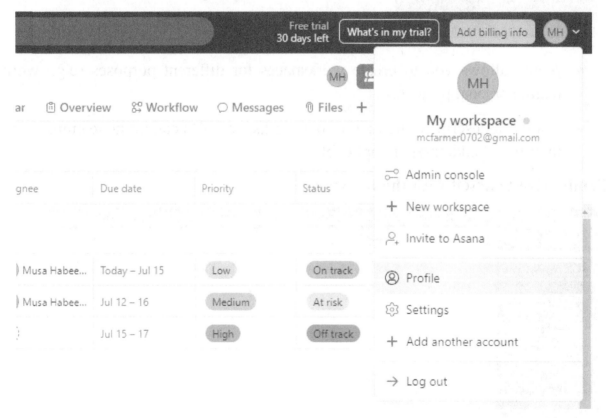

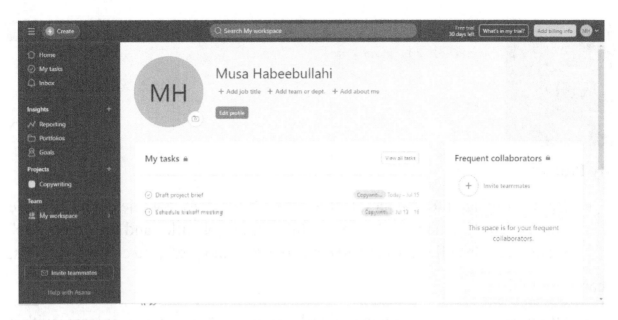

Additional Tips:

- Use the search bar at the top for finding specific projects, tasks, or teammates.

- Consider integrating Asana with your preferred productivity tools to streamline workflows (available on paid plans).

- Experiment with Asana's functionalities to discover how it best meets your project management needs.

By following these steps, you'll effectively set up your Asana account and begin leveraging its features for organized and efficient project management. Remember, Asana provides ample resources and tutorials to support you throughout your journey.

Understanding Asana Interface

In this guide, you'll discover how to efficiently navigate Asana and gain a thorough understanding of its interface. Here's a breakdown of key features and how to use them effectively:

Top Bar:

The top bar in Asana remains constant across all pages and consists of three main components: My profile, search, and Quick add:

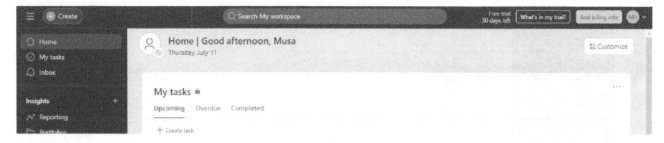

My Profile:

- Before diving into Asana's features, it's crucial to complete your profile details. This includes adding your full name, job title, and an "about me" section to help colleagues understand your role and preferred contact methods.

Search for Objects:

- Utilize the search function to find tasks, projects, tags, people, or teams within your workspace or organization. You can perform basic searches by typing keywords into the search bar, or use advanced search filters for more specific results. Saved searches can also be created for easy access in the future.

Quick Add Button:

- Found conveniently throughout Asana, the **Quick add** button allows you to swiftly create tasks, projects, messages, teams, or invite team members to Asana.

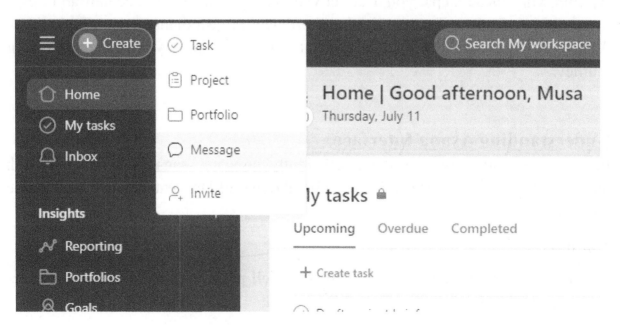

Managing Your Work on the Sidebar:

- Home: Customize your Home to focus on tasks with approaching deadlines, recent projects, or goal progress tracking. You can adjust your Home setup at any time. To access Home, click **Home** from the side bar.

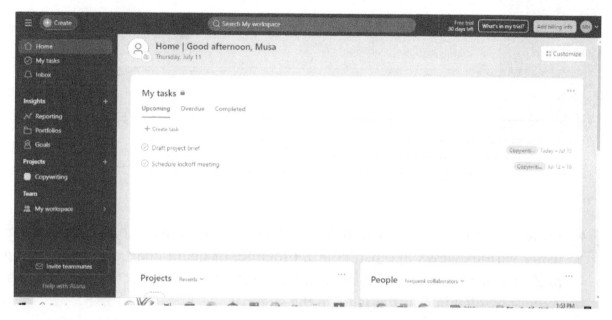

- My Tasks: Access all tasks assigned to you in Asana. Prioritize your workload effectively by sorting tasks by due date or organizing them into sections. To access, click **My Tasks** from the sidebar.

- Inbox: Your notification center where you receive updates on tasks and projects you're involved in. Manage notifications and take actions such as archiving or creating follow-up tasks directly from the Inbox. Click **Inbox** from the side bar to access it.

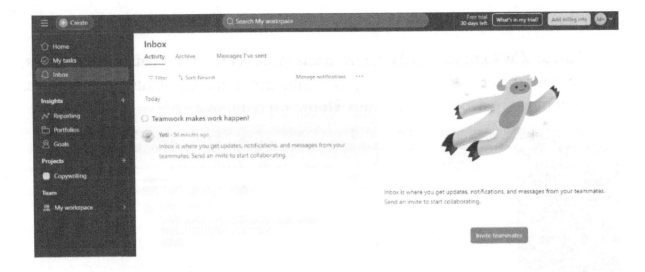

Projects and Teams:

- Projects: Capture team workflows, from product roadmaps to event planning, using various views like list, board, timeline, or Gantt chart. Access existing projects, star favorites for quick access, and create new projects and portfolios. Access by clicking on **Projects** in the side bar.

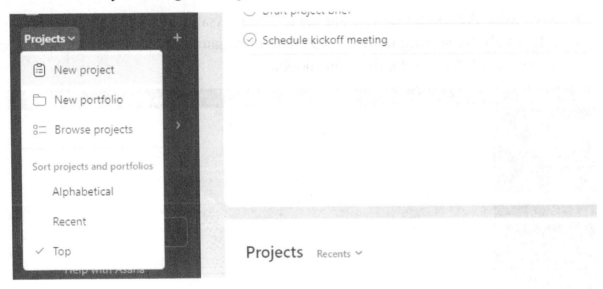

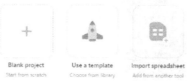

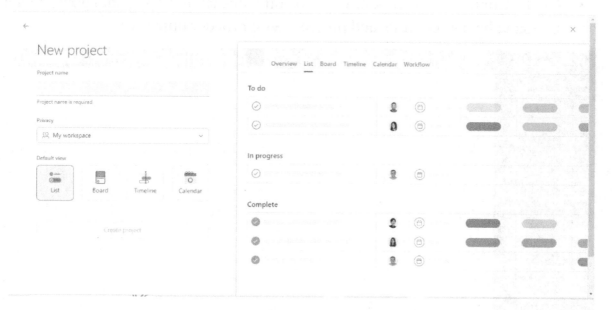

- Teams: Collaborate with specific groups within your organization. Teams have their own members, admins, projects, messages, and calendars, providing efficient collaboration and project management. Click **Teams** in the side bar to access it.

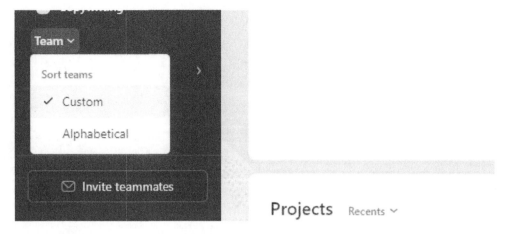

Insights:

- Goals: Connect your work directly to company, team, or personal goals. Goals in Asana help align tasks and projects with broader objectives.

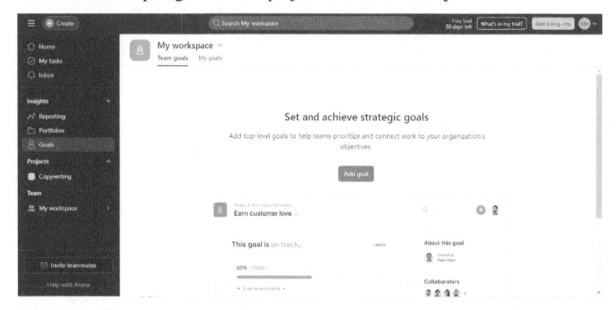

- Reporting: Visualize real-time data with customizable dashboards, offering insights into project progress and team performance.

  ➢ Workload: Manage team capacity and workload allocation visually, ensuring balanced work distribution and effective planning.

- Portfolios: Group related projects together and monitor their health in real-time. Portfolios act as centralized folders for critical projects, offering detailed insights and updates on progress.

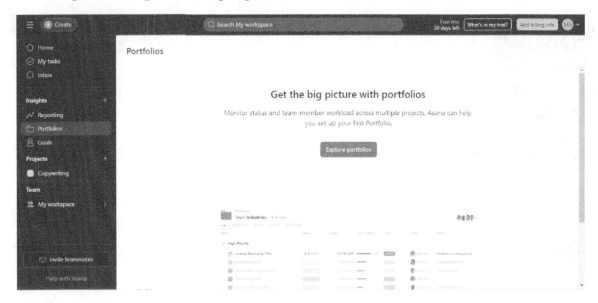

By mastering these features, you'll navigate Asana proficiently, enhancing collaboration, productivity, and project management efficiency within your team or organization.

Importing Data and Setting Up Your Team

Importing data and setting up your team in Asana are pivotal steps to streamline workflows and foster effective collaboration. Here's a comprehensive guide to get started:

Importing Data:

Prepare Your Data:

- Organize your data in a compatible format such as CSV or spreadsheet, ensuring it includes essential details like task names, assignees, due dates, and project associations.

Access Import Options:

- Navigate to the project in Asana where you wish to import data.

- Click on the project options (represented by a dropdown symbol) and select "Import."

- Choose the file format (CSV or spreadsheet) and follow the on-screen instructions to upload your file.

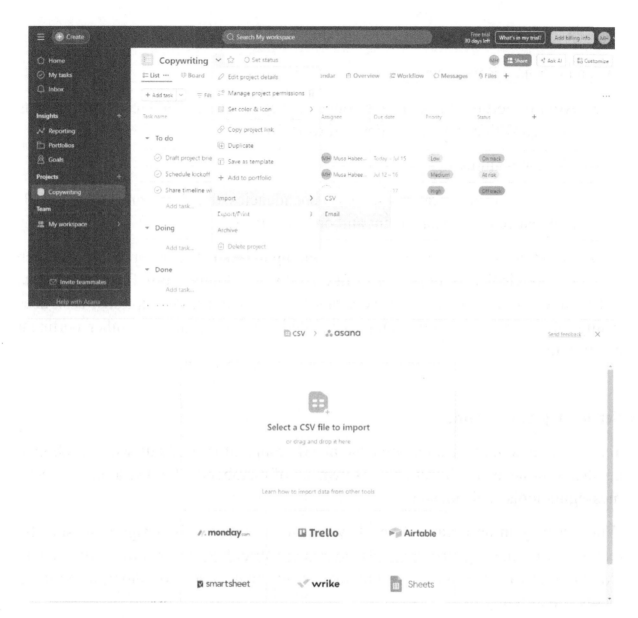

Mapping Fields:

- Asana will guide you through mapping fields from your imported file to corresponding Asana fields (e.g., task name, assignee).

- Verify and adjust mappings as necessary to maintain data accuracy and relevance in Asana.

Review and Confirm:

- Review the imported data to ensure accuracy and completeness.

- Confirm the import to populate tasks, projects, or other items within Asana.

- Post-Import Adjustments:

Task and Project Refinement:

- After importing, fine-tune task details, project settings, and team assignments to align with current priorities and workflows.

Utilize Asana Features:

- Leverage Asana's features such as dependencies, due dates, and custom fields to enhance task management and organization.

CSV Importer: This feature is ideal for bringing in task lists from spreadsheets such as Excel, Google Sheets, or platforms like Trello and Monday.com. Ensure your data is formatted in a CSV file with columns for task names, descriptions, assignees (using email addresses), due dates (formatted correctly), and any other pertinent information.

Setting Up Your Team:

Teams within an organization are designated groups of individuals who collaborate on shared projects. Each team has its own set of members, administrators, projects, messaging tools, and calendar.

When users join an organization, they are not automatically assigned to specific teams within that organization. Instead, users can either create new teams or join existing ones. It's possible for a member of an organization to belong to multiple teams concurrently.

Locating Teams:

- If you are a member of an organization, you will find two lists of teams in the sidebar. One list includes teams you are currently a member of, while the other lists teams you can explore, join, or request to join.

- If a member has access restricted to a particular project within the organization, their sidebar will display only the teams they have access to. They won't be able to view other teams within the organization.

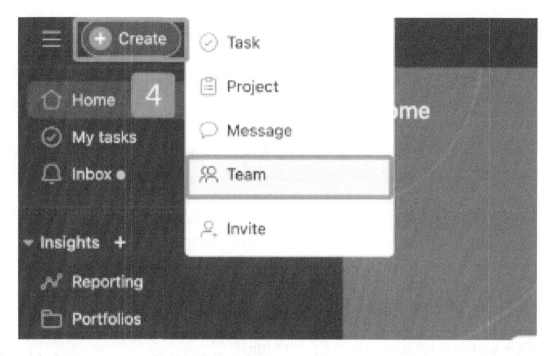

In the side bar, you can do the following:

- See teams you belong to and access your team's page.

- Create a new team.

- Explore and join other teams within the organization.

- Quickly create a team using the quick add button.

Team Page:

The team page serves as a centralized hub where you can manage your team's work. It consists of three tabs: Overview, Messages, and Calendar.

Overview:

In the Overview tab, you can do the following:

- View the team's description.

- Manage team members and their roles.

- Access and create new projects associated with the team.

- Utilize project templates and create new ones.

Managing Team Projects:

- The Projects section displays all projects linked with your team.

- Create new projects, search for existing ones, and manage both active and archived projects.

Organizing Projects:

- Pin important projects to the top of your list for quicker access.

- Reorganize pinned projects by dragging them into desired order.

Using Messages:

- Messages allow for team-wide communication, including announcements and discussions spanning multiple projects.

- Send new messages to team members and review previous communications.

Team Calendar:

- Team calendars consolidate tasks from all team projects, offering visibility into ongoing and upcoming work.

- Navigate through different months or years, return to the current week or month, and toggle weekends on or off.

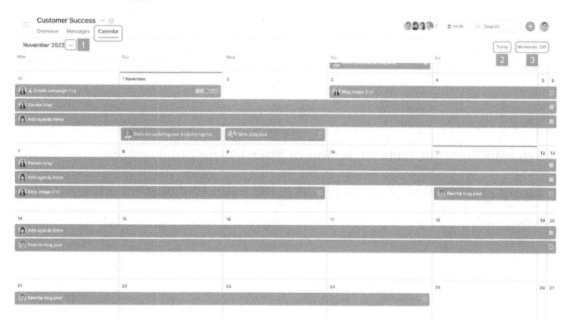

Note: Team calendars are read-only, meaning tasks cannot be added directly to them. Tasks must be added to specific projects to appear on the team's calendar view.

Create a New Team:

Start collaborating with colleagues in your organization by creating a new team. You can initiate this process through your admin console, sidebar, or quick add button.

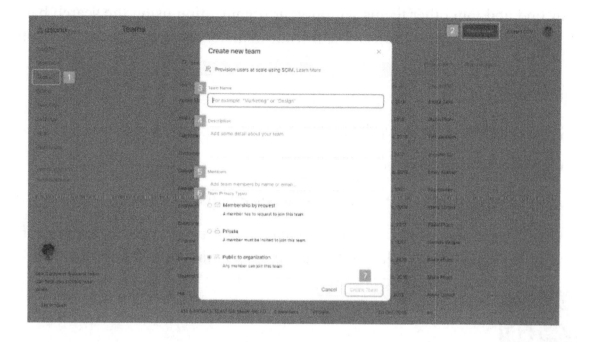

To create a team via the admin console:

- Navigate to 'Teams' in your admin console sidebar.

- Click on the 'Create team' button located in the top-right corner.

- A popup window will appear prompting you to enter your team's name and description.

- Add team members and set privacy preferences.

- Click 'Create team.'

Note: You can invite multiple members at once by pasting email addresses from a CSV file into the invite window.

Creating a team via the quick add button:

- Click on the quick 'add (+)' button at the top-left of your screen.

- Select 'Team.'

- Fill out all required fields in the pop-up window and click 'Create Team.'

- After creating a team, you automatically become the team admin. You can adjust permissions and settings at any time.

Join a Team:

You can find and join other teams within your organization using the search bar. If you want to collaborate on projects with team members, you can request to join a team.

To request to join a team:

- Search for the team using the search bar.

- Click on the team and request to join if necessary.

- Alternatively, you can receive an invite via email or a shareable link.

- Once you request to join, an existing team member will need to approve your request. Public teams allow automatic membership without approval.

To approve membership requests:

- Click on the three-dot icon next to the team's name.

- Select 'Approve Pending Members.'

- Review requests and choose to approve or deny each request.

Team Settings:

Access your team's settings to manage its details, including name changes, permissions, members, notifications, and deletion.

To access team settings:

- Click on the team name in the sidebar to open the team page.

- Click the drop-down arrow next to the team's name.

- Select 'Edit team settings.'

Team settings are divided into three tabs: General, Members, and Advanced

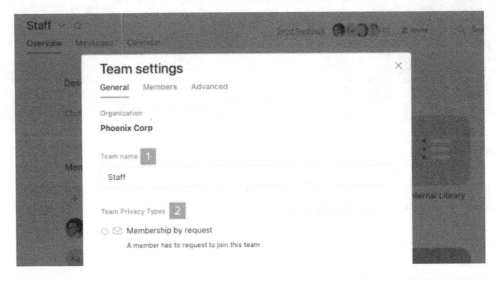

General:

- Change the team's name.

- Adjust privacy settings.

Members:

- View and manage team members and their project access.

- Invite new members and remove existing ones.

Advanced:

- Manage editing and membership controls (admins only).

- Activate integrations like 'Harvest.'

- Delete the team (note: members will receive notification).

When removing members from a team, they retain access to their assigned tasks unless removed from the organization entirely.

If you use Asana Goals, make sure to reassign any goals associated with the team to another suitable team before deleting it. This step will enable you to easily locate these goals by filtering them under the newly assigned team.

Deleting a team will result in the removal of all its projects, including those with different privacy settings such as those visible only to team members, which you might not have access to.

Move Project to Another Team:

You can move projects to other teams where you are a member.

To move a project:

- Click the drop-down arrow on the project.

- Select 'Edit project details.'

In 'Select a team,' type the name of the destination team.

CHAPTER THREE
CREATING AND MANAGING PROJECTS

Organizing Projects with Workspaces, Teams and Tags

Creating and Using Workspaces:

Setting Up a Workspace

- Access Workspaces: Click on your profile picture in the top right corner and select "New Workspace."

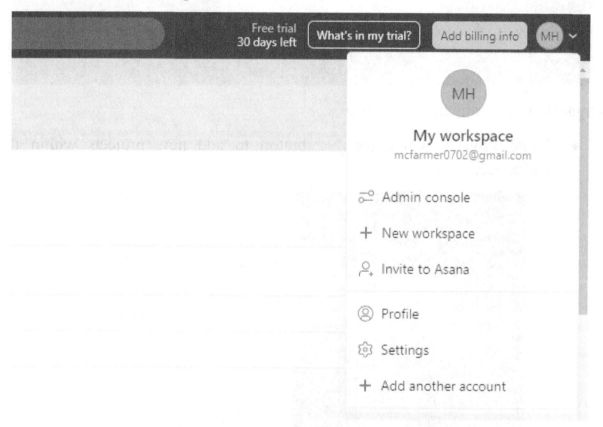

- Name the Workspace: Choose a name that reflects the focus, such as "Marketing Department" or "Client Projects."

- Invite Members: Add team members by entering their email addresses.

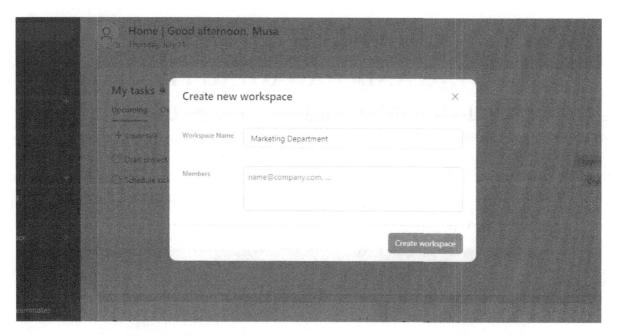

Organize Projects in the Workspace:

- Create Projects: Click the "+" button to add new projects within the workspace.

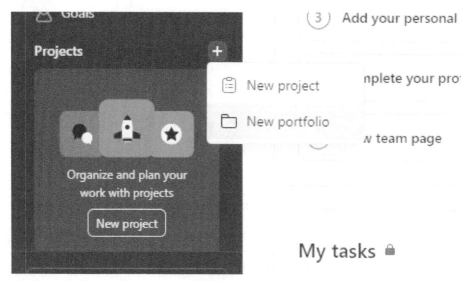

- Structure Tasks: Within each project, break down the work into tasks and subtasks.

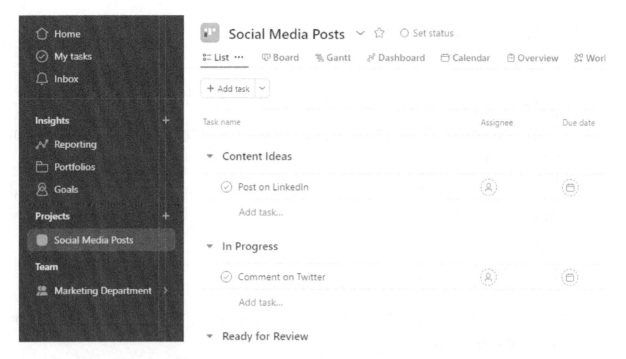

- Assign Tasks: Allocate tasks to team members and set due dates to ensure accountability.

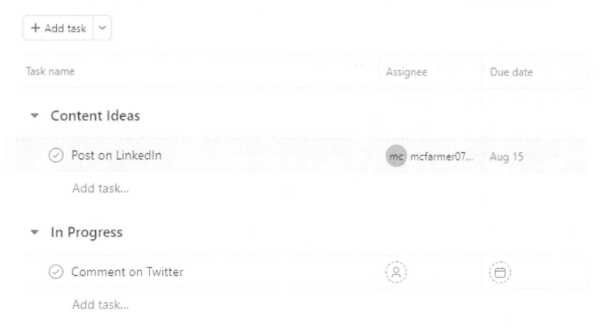

Forming and Managing Teams:

Establishing a Team:

- Navigate to Teams: Go to the Teams section in the admin console or sidebar.

- Create a Team: Click the "Create Team" button and fill in details like the team name and description.

- Add Members: Invite team members by entering their email addresses and setting permissions.

Organize Projects Within Teams:

- Assign Projects: Assign relevant projects to the appropriate teams.

- Access the Team Page: Manage the team's projects, messages, and calendar from the team page.

- Pin Key Projects: Pin important projects to the top of the team's project list for easy access.

Utilizing Tags for Better Organization:

Creating and Applying Tags:

- Create Tags: Add tags to tasks while creating or editing them, indicating status, priority, or type.

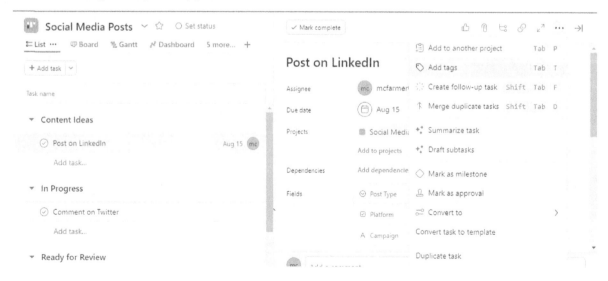

- Apply Tags: Use tags like "High Priority," "Bug," or "In Progress" to categorize tasks.

Filtering and Searching with Tags:

- Filter by Tags: Use the search bar to filter tasks based on tags, making it easier to find tasks across projects.

- Save Tag Views: Save filtered views for quick access in the future to improve task tracking and management.

Additional Tips for Organization:

- Use Templates: Create project templates for recurring workflows to save time and ensure consistency.

- Add Custom Fields: Incorporate custom fields to tasks for extra details like budget, project phase, or client name.

- Review and Adjust Regularly: Periodically review your workspaces, teams, and tags to ensure they meet your organizational needs and make adjustments as needed.

By implementing these steps, you can effectively organize your projects in Asana, enhancing collaboration and productivity.

Setting Project Goals, Due Dates and Custom Fields

Establishing Project Goals:

Define the Project Scope:

- Set the Objective: Identify the main goal of the project.

- Break Down the Goal: Divide the main goal into smaller, actionable steps.

Create Goals in Asana:

- Navigate to the desired project in your Asana workspace.

- Click on the three dots menu in the top right corner of the project window.

- Select "Add Goal" from the menu options.

- Specify Goals: Ensure goals are clear, measurable, and time-bound.

Assign Responsibilities:

- Allocate Goal Owners: Assign each goal to a team member.

- Set Milestones: Establish intermediate checkpoints to track progress.

Setting Due Dates:

Determine Due Dates:

- Define Timelines: Set realistic deadlines for tasks and goals.

- Prioritize Tasks: Identify key tasks and assign earlier due dates to ensure timely completion.

Set Due Dates in Asana:

- Open the Task: Click on the task to assign a due date.

- Select the Date: Use the calendar icon to choose the appropriate due date.

- Regularly Review: Adjust due dates based on project progress and any changes.

Monitor Deadlines:

- Track Overdue Tasks: Utilize Asana's features to identify and address overdue tasks.

- Set Reminders: Enable notifications and reminders for upcoming deadlines.

Adding Custom Fields:

Identify Necessary Data:

- Determine Additional Information: Identify what extra data is needed for tasks and projects, such as budget, priority, project phase, or client name.

Create Custom Fields in Asana:

- Open the Project: Go to the project where custom fields will be added.

- Access Project Settings: Click on the project and select "Customize" at the top-right corner of the project page.

- Add Custom Fields: Choose "Fields" either under the "Edit" or "Add" options, and define the field type (e.g., text, number, dropdown).

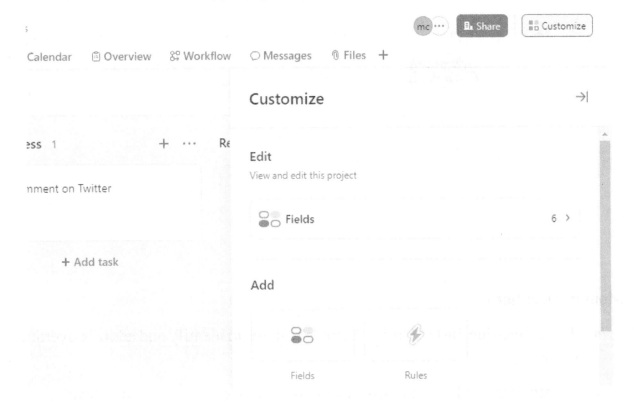

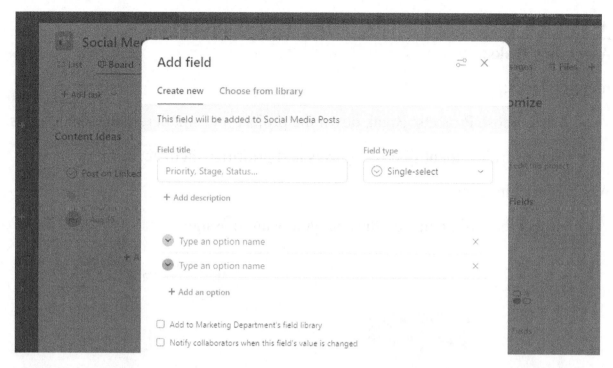

Populate Custom Fields:

- Input Data: Enter relevant information into the custom fields for each task.

- Use Templates: Create templates with predefined custom fields for consistent use across similar projects.

Utilize Custom Fields for Tracking and Reporting:

- Filter and Sort: Use custom fields to filter and sort tasks, aiding in progress tracking and workload management.

- Generate Reports: Create reports using custom fields to analyse project performance and make informed decisions.

By following these steps, you can effectively establish project goals, set due dates, and utilize custom fields in Asana to improve project management and team collaboration.

Assigning Tasks and Collaborating with Teammates

Assigning Tasks:

Identify Tasks:

- Decompose Projects: Break down the project into smaller, manageable tasks.

- Set Priorities: Identify critical tasks and prioritize them accordingly.

Assign Tasks in Asana:

- Select the Task: Click on the task you want to assign.

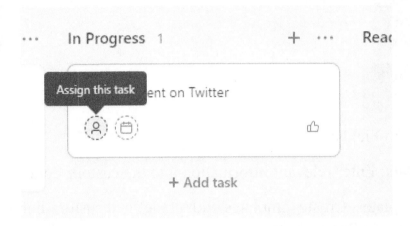

- Assign a Team Member: Use the assignee field to designate the appropriate team member.

- Set Due Dates: Establish realistic deadlines to keep the project on schedule.

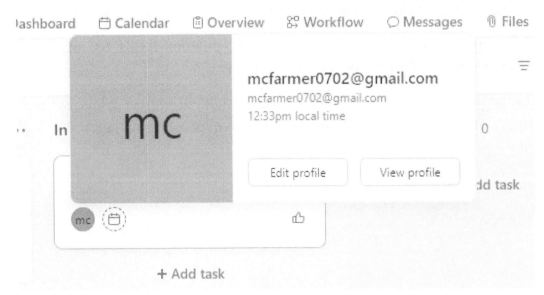

Provide Detailed Descriptions:

- Add Instructions: Include clear and comprehensive instructions for completing the task.

- Attach Files: Upload relevant documents or files to the task for easy reference.

Collaborating with Teammates:

Use Task Comments:

- Direct Communication: Use the comment section within tasks to communicate with assigned team members.

- Tag Teammates: Mention teammates using the @ symbol to ensure they receive notifications.

Share Updates and Feedback:

- Regular Updates: Keep the team informed about progress by sharing updates within the task comments.

- Provide Feedback: Offer constructive feedback and acknowledge completed work.

Utilize Team Messages:

- Announcements: Use team messages to share important announcements or updates that affect the entire team.

- Project Discussions: Engage in discussions that span multiple projects or tasks.

Monitoring and Adjusting Tasks:

Track Task Progress:

- Review Status: Regularly check the status of tasks to ensure they are on track.

- Use Project Views: Utilize different views (e.g., list, board, calendar) in Asana for a comprehensive overview of task progress.

Reassign Tasks if Necessary:

- Monitor Workload: Keep an eye on team members' workloads and reassign tasks if someone is overloaded.

- Adjust Due Dates: Modify due dates based on task progress and any changes.

Hold Regular Meetings:

- Conduct Check-ins: Regularly hold team meetings to discuss progress, address issues, and plan next steps.

- Foster Collaboration: Encourage team members to share ideas and ask for help when needed.

Utilizing Asana Features for Collaboration:

Use Project Conversations:

- Initiate Discussions: Use the project conversation feature to start discussions related to the entire project.

- Share Ideas: Encourage team members to share ideas and feedback within the project conversation thread.

Integrate with Other Tools:

- Connect Apps: Integrate Asana with other tools your team uses (e.g., Slack, Google Drive) to streamline communication and collaboration.

- Automate Workflows: Utilize Asana's automation features to handle repetitive tasks and notifications.

Review and Reflect:

- Conduct Retrospectives: After completing projects, hold retrospective meetings to discuss what went well and areas for improvement.

- Document Learnings: Record key learnings and best practices to improve future collaboration and project management.

By implementing these steps, you can effectively assign tasks and collaborate with your teammates in Asana, ensuring smooth project execution and enhanced team coordination.

CHAPTER FOUR
CREATING AND MANAGING TASKS

Different Task Types

Asana offers different task types to help you organize and manage projects more effectively. Here are the key task types and how they can be used:

Standard Tasks:

- Overview: Basic tasks for tracking work that needs to be done.

- Examples: Everyday work items, routine tasks, individual to-dos.

- Features: Assign to team members, set due dates, add subtasks, attachments, and comments.

Subtasks:

- Overview: Smaller components of a larger task.

- Examples: Breaking down a complex task into simpler steps.

- Features: Can be assigned, have due dates, and detailed descriptions, similar to standard tasks.

Milestones:

- Overview: Key points in a project timeline indicating significant achievements.

- Examples: Major project deliverables, phase completions, significant events.

- Features: Marked with a diamond icon to signify important progress points.

Sections:

- Overview: Organizational units within a project to group related tasks.

- Examples: Stages of a project, types of tasks, prioritization categories.

- Features: Helps organize tasks for better clarity and structure.

Recurring Tasks:

- Overview: Tasks that need to be repeated at regular intervals.

- Examples: Weekly meetings, monthly reports, daily updates.

- Features: Set to repeat on a daily, weekly, monthly basis, or at custom intervals.

Approval Tasks:

- Overview: Tasks that require formal approval before completion.

- Examples: Reviewing documents, approving designs, budget approvals.

- Features: Special approval status, can be accepted or rejected by designated approvers.

Dependent Tasks:

- Overview: Tasks that rely on the completion of other tasks.

- Examples: Sequential workflows, where one task must be done before another starts.

- Features: Links to predecessor tasks, helping visualize dependencies and plan timelines.

Task Templates:

- Overview: Pre-defined structures for recurring tasks.

- Examples: Standard procedures, routine project steps.

- Features: Reusable templates for consistent task setup across projects.

Custom Fields Tasks:

- Overview: Tasks with additional fields for specific information.

- Examples: Tracking budget, priority, project phase, client details.

- Features: Custom fields to capture unique data points for better tracking and reporting.

Adding Descriptions, Attachments and Dependencies to Tasks

Adding Descriptions to Tasks:

Objective: Ensure team members fully understand the task by providing clear, detailed information.

How to Add Descriptions:

- Open the Task: Click on the task to view its details pane.

- Enter Description: Type a detailed explanation in the description field, including necessary instructions, goals, or context.

- Format Text: Use formatting options (bold, italics, bullet points) to enhance readability.

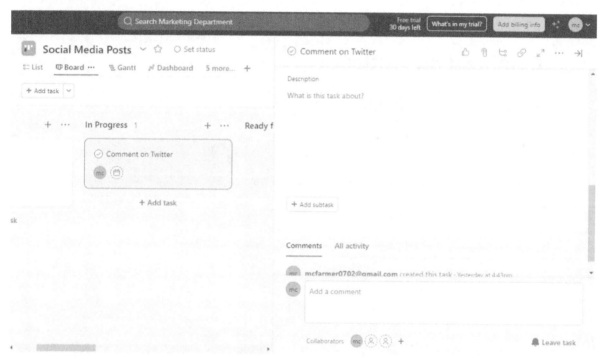

Note:

- Be clear and concise.

- Provide step-by-step instructions if needed.

- Highlight key information.

Adding Attachments to Tasks:

Objective: Provide all necessary resources for completing the task by attaching relevant documents, images, or files.

How to Add Attachments:

- Open the Task: Click on the task to view its details pane.

- Attach Files: Click the "Paperclip" icon or drag and drop files into the task pane.

- Choose Source: Attach files from your computer, cloud storage (e.g., Google Drive, Dropbox), or add web links.

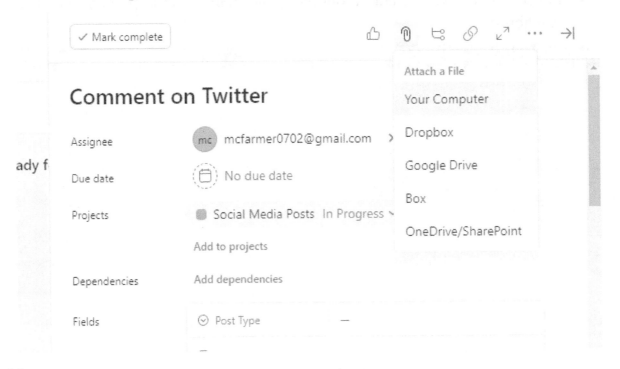

Note:

- Ensure attachments are relevant and clearly labelled.

- Attach the most current versions of files to avoid confusion.

- Use file-sharing links for large documents.

Adding Dependencies to Tasks:

Objective: Create relationships between tasks to indicate that one task depends on the completion of another, ensuring a proper workflow sequence.

How to Add Dependencies:

- Open the Task: Click on the task you want to set as dependent.

- Set Dependency: Find "Dependencies" and select "Add Dependency."

- Choose Preceding Task: Find and select the task that this task depends on.

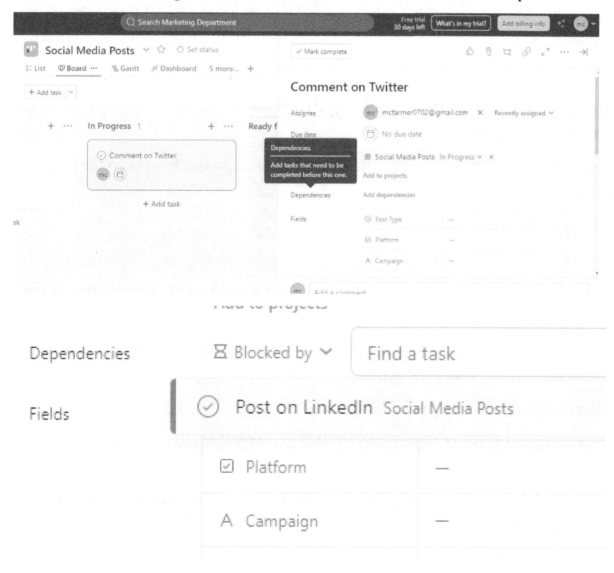

Tips:

- Clearly define task dependencies to prevent bottlenecks.

- Regularly review dependencies to ensure they remain relevant.

- Use dependencies to effectively manage project timelines.

Summary:

By adding detailed descriptions, relevant attachments, and setting task dependencies in Asana, you can improve task clarity, provide necessary resources, and maintain an organized workflow. This enhances project management and fosters better team collaboration.

Prioritizing Tasks and Tracking Progress
Prioritizing Tasks:

Goal: Ensure key tasks are identified and addressed promptly to keep the project on track.

Methods for Prioritizing Tasks:

Evaluate Task Importance:

- Identify Crucial Tasks: Find tasks that significantly impact the project's success.

- Assess Urgency: Consider deadlines and dependencies to determine which tasks need immediate action.

Utilize Asana's Priority Tools:

- Custom Fields: Create custom fields to categorize tasks by priority levels like "High," "Medium," or "Low."

- Tags: Apply tags to highlight priority levels, making tasks easily identifiable in lists.

Organize Tasks Effectively:

- Sections: Divide tasks into sections based on their priority within projects.

- Sorting: Use Asana's sorting options to arrange tasks by priority or due date.

Best Practices:

- Regularly review and update task priorities.

- Communicate changes in priorities to the team to ensure alignment.

Monitoring Progress:

Goal: Keep track of task and project progress to ensure timely completion and promptly address any issues.

Methods for Tracking Progress:

Leverage Asana Views:

- List View: Get a detailed overview of tasks, their statuses, and assignees.

- Board View: Visualize tasks in columns representing different stages of completion.

- Calendar View: See tasks and deadlines on a calendar for effective timeline management.

- Timeline View: Create Gantt charts to map out project schedules and track dependencies.

Status Updates:

- Task Status: Regularly update task statuses (e.g., "In Progress," "Completed").

- Progress Reports: Generate and share progress reports using Asana's reporting features.

Check-ins and Milestones:

- Regular Check-ins: Schedule regular team meetings to review progress and address any issues.

- Milestones: Set and track milestones to mark significant achievements within the project.

Dashboards and Charts:

- Create Dashboards: Use Asana's dashboards for a real-time overview of project metrics and performance.

- Visual Reports: Utilize charts and graphs to visualize task completion rates, workload distribution, and other key metrics.

Best Practices:

- Encourage team members to regularly update task statuses and provide feedback.

Use automation features to send reminders for upcoming deadlines or overdue tasks.

CHAPTER FIVE
COMMUNICATION AND COLLABORATION IN ASANA

Using Comments and Mentions for Effective Communication
Using Comments:

Goal: Enhance communication within tasks, keeping all team members informed and coordinated.

Steps to Use Comments:

Open the Task:

- Select the task where you need to add a comment.

Write Your Comment:

- Type your message in the comment field, including any necessary details or updates.

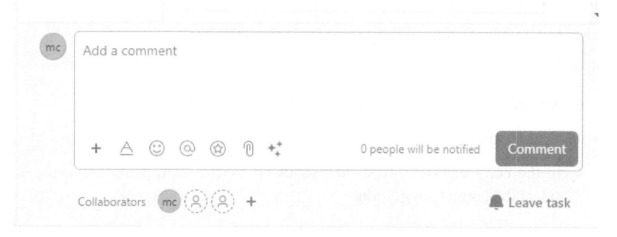

Attach Files:

- If applicable, attach relevant documents or files to provide additional context.

Post the Comment:

- Click "Post" to share your comment with task assignees and followers.

Tips for Effective Comments:

- Keep your comments clear and concise to prevent misunderstandings.

- Use bullet points or numbered lists to organize information.

- Provide sufficient context so everyone understands the significance of your comment.

Utilizing Mentions:

Goal: Ensure specific team members receive important comments or updates immediately.

Steps to Use Mentions:

Open the Task:

- Navigate to the task where you want to mention a colleague.

Write Your Comment:

- In the comment field, type "@" followed by the team member's name and select the correct suggestion.

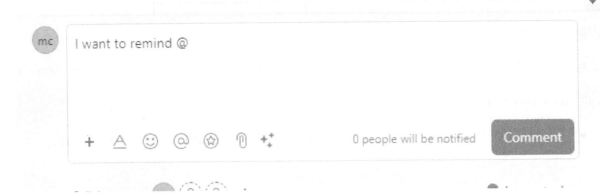

Compose Your Message:

- Continue writing your message, directly addressing the mentioned team member or seeking their input.

Post the Comment:

- Click "Post" to notify the mentioned team member.

Tips for Effective Mentions:

- Mention only those who need to be involved to avoid excessive notifications.

- Clearly state why you are mentioning the person, whether for input, approval, or an update.

- Combine mentions with specific, actionable requests to ensure clarity.

Tips for Effective Communication:

- Respond Promptly: Address comments and mentions quickly to keep the project moving.

- Maintain Organization: Keep discussions within relevant tasks to preserve context.

- Encourage Participation: Create an environment where team members feel comfortable providing feedback and asking questions.

- Use Emojis: Add emojis to convey tone and make communication more engaging.

Using comments and mentions effectively in Asana enhances team communication, keeps everyone updated, and ensures smooth project progress. Clear, timely, and well-organized communication boosts collaboration and project success.

Task Approval and Feedback Mechanism

Objective: Implement a systematic approach to review and approve tasks, ensuring they meet quality standards and align with project objectives.

Steps for Task Review and Approval:

Define Approval Criteria:

- Clearly outline the conditions under which a task is considered ready for approval, such as completeness, quality standards, or adherence to guidelines.

Assign Reviewers:

- Identify responsible individuals, such as project managers, team leads, or stakeholders, who will review and approve tasks.

Approval Decision:

- Reviewers evaluate tasks and decide whether to approve them for completion or request revisions.

Task Status Update:

Once approved, update the task status to reflect its current stage, like "Approved" or "Completed."

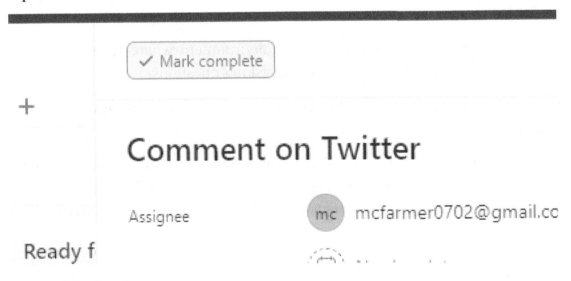

Feedback Mechanism:

Provide Constructive Feedback:

- Comment on tasks to offer feedback, suggestions, or corrections aimed at improving task outcomes.

Utilize Mentions for Feedback:

- Notify task assignees or relevant team members directly using mentions (@) to ensure timely receipt of feedback.

Encourage Dialogue:

- Foster an environment where team members can discuss feedback, ask questions, and seek clarification within task comments.

Best Practices for Task Review and Feedback:

- Clarity and Transparency: Clearly communicate approval criteria to avoid confusion and ensure consistency.

- Prompt Responses: Provide feedback promptly to maintain task progress and address issues efficiently.

- Documentation: Document approvals and feedback within Asana to maintain a clear record of decisions and improvements.

Implementing a structured task review and approval process in Asana enhances task quality and alignment with project goals. Clear criteria, timely feedback, and open communication channels contribute to improved collaboration and project success.

Utilizing Asana for Team Discussions and Meetings

Initiating and Managing Team Discussions:

Starting Team Discussions:

Accessing Project Conversations:

- Open the project where you wish to initiate a discussion.

Starting a Discussion:

- Utilize Asana's project conversation feature to commence a new thread for discussion.

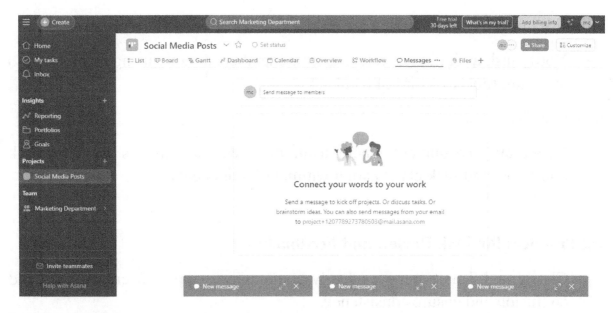

Inviting Participants:

- Notify team members by mentioning them with @mentions to encourage their participation.

Managing Discussions:

Maintaining Focus and Context:

- Ensure discussions stay on-topic, focusing on specific tasks or project milestones to maintain clarity.

Organizing Threads:

- Use threaded replies to structure related comments and maintain organized discussions.

Recording Decisions:

- Document important decisions, updates, or insights within the discussion thread for future reference.

Scheduling and Managing Team Meetings:

Creating Meeting Tasks:

- Use Asana tasks to create and schedule meetings, setting dates, times, and agendas.

Assigning Action Items:

- Assign tasks to team members based on meeting outcomes and identified action items.

Setting Reminders:

- Enable reminders and notifications to ensure all participants are informed about upcoming meetings and tasks.

Conducting Effective Team Meetings:

Preparing Meeting Agendas:

- Develop and share meeting agendas in Asana to outline topics, objectives, and discussion points.

Recording Meeting Notes:

- Document meeting notes, decisions, and action items in real-time using Asana tasks or comments.

Following Up on Action Items:

- Assign tasks and deadlines for action items identified during meetings to track progress and ensure accountability.

Enhancing Collaboration:

Integrating External Tools:

- Connect Asana with tools like Slack or Google Workspace to facilitate seamless file sharing and communication during meetings.

Promoting Engagement:

- Encourage active participation and feedback from team members to foster collaboration and idea sharing.

Reviewing and Documenting:

Reviewing Meeting History:

- Refer back to past meeting notes and discussions in Asana to monitor progress and maintain continuity.

Documenting Decisions and Progress:

- Maintain a comprehensive record of decisions, progress updates, and milestones achieved within Asana for future reference and reporting.

Following these steps enables teams to effectively utilize Asana for team discussions and meetings, promoting collaboration, ensuring clear communication, and enhancing overall project management efficiency.

Well-defined agendas, structured discussions, and documented outcomes contribute to increased team productivity and successful project outcomes.

CHAPTER SIX
ASANA FOR EFFICIENT WORKFLOW
Creating Templates for Repetitive Tasks

Asana enables you to save time and ensure consistency by creating templates for recurring tasks. Here's a comprehensive guide to help you get started:

Identify Repetitive Tasks:

- Identify tasks that frequently occur across your projects and share similar steps and requirements, making them suitable for templating.

- Examples include client onboarding checklists, social media post creation processes, or bug reporting procedures.

Craft the Template Task:

Create a new task in Asana that will serve as the foundation for your template. Include essential details such as:

- Task Name: Choose a descriptive name that clearly defines the purpose (e.g., "Social Media Post Creation").

- Description: Outline the steps involved in the task to provide guidance for template users.

- Assignee: If applicable, assign a default assignee within the template.

- Subtasks: Break down the task into smaller, actionable steps using subtasks, each with clear descriptions.

- Attachments: Attach relevant documents, resources, or checklists needed for future instances of the task.

Convert to Template:

After setting up your template task with all necessary details, access the task menu (typically represented by three dots).

Choose "Convert to Template" from the menu options. This action transforms your task into a reusable template within Asana.

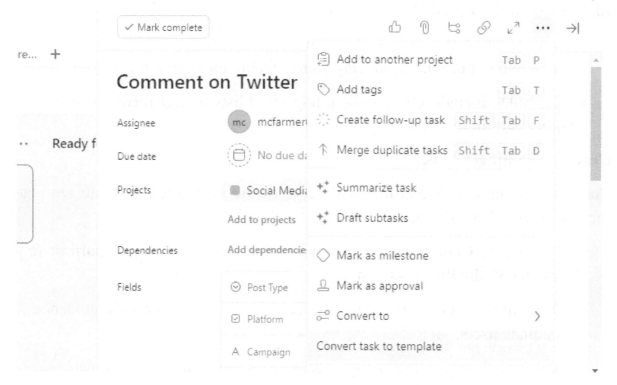

To add a template:

- Click on the "Customize" option.

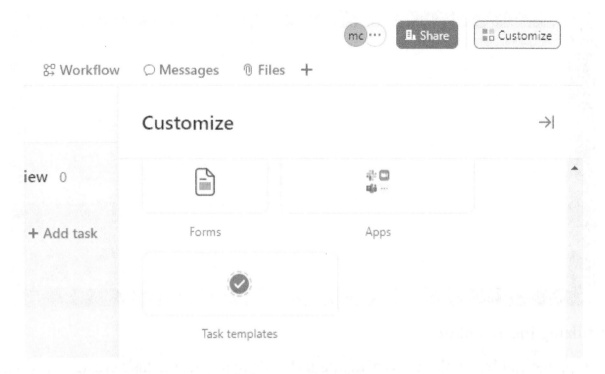

- Scroll down and choose "Task template."

Task templates

Utilizing the Template:

Templates can be employed to generate tasks using any of the task creation options available within your project. To access task templates within a project, click on the 'Add new' dropdown or on the '+' button next to your section headers. This action will reveal an additional dropdown menu containing all task templates relevant to the project.

- From the Add new dropdown menu:

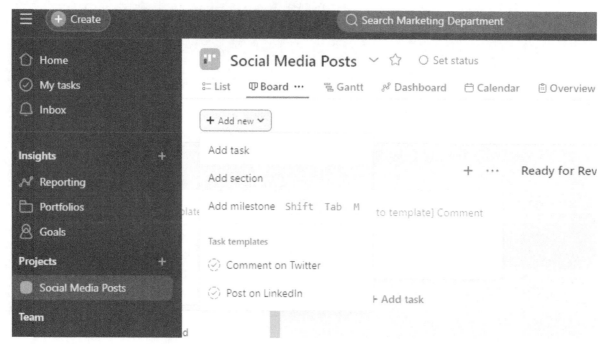

- Using the "+" icon:

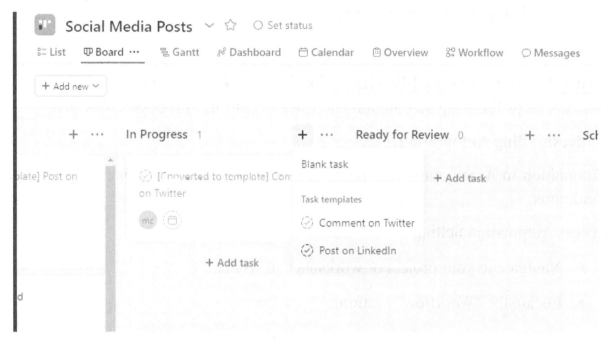

Additional Tips:

- Organize Your Templates: Use folders or tags in Asana to categorize templates for easy access and management.

- Template Permissions (For Teams): In team environments, manage permissions to control who can create and modify templates, ensuring consistency.

- Keep Templates Updated: Regularly review and update templates to reflect changes in processes or improvements in repetitive tasks.

By leveraging Asana's templating feature, you can:

- Save Time: Avoid starting tasks from scratch, allowing more focus on project-specific details.

- Ensure Consistency: Maintain standardized approaches across projects for repetitive tasks.

- Enhance Efficiency: Streamline workflows and boost overall team productivity.

- Empower your team to prioritize project goals by harnessing Asana's templating functionality effectively.

Using Constraints and Resizing for Design Flexibility

Here are steps for using automation and rules to optimize processes in Asana:

Understanding Automation:

Automation in Asana automates repetitive tasks based on predefined triggers and conditions.

Access Automation Settings:

- Navigate to your project or workspace in Asana.

- Locate the "Workflow" section.

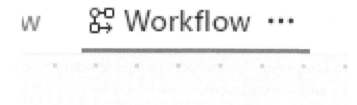

Create Automations:

- Click on "Workflow" to start creating a new automation.

- Choose the type of automation you need, such as task assignments, due date reminders, status updates, or notifications.

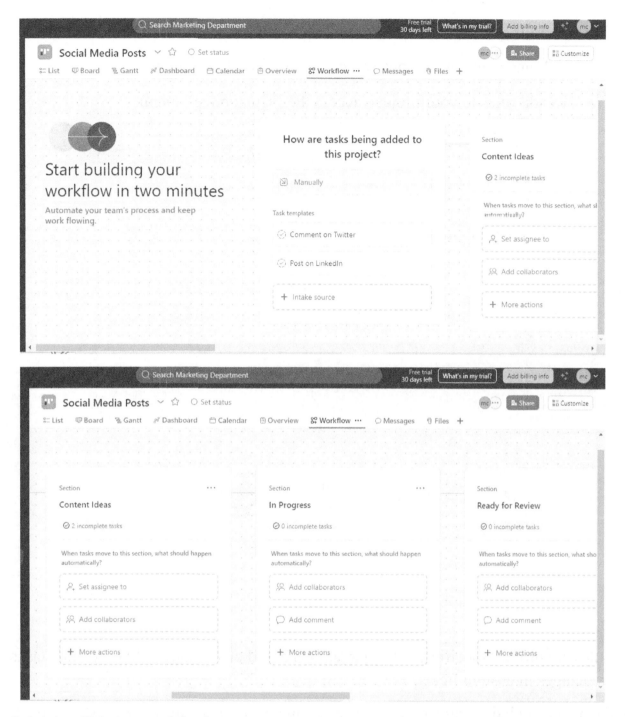

Selecting Triggers and Actions:

- Define trigger conditions for the automation to initiate, like task creation, approaching due dates, or updates to specific fields.

- Specify the actions Asana should automatically perform when triggers are met, such as assigning tasks, updating statuses, sending notifications, or modifying custom fields.

Understanding Rules:

Rules in Asana automate actions when specific conditions are met.

- To add rules to your project, access the "Customize" menu.

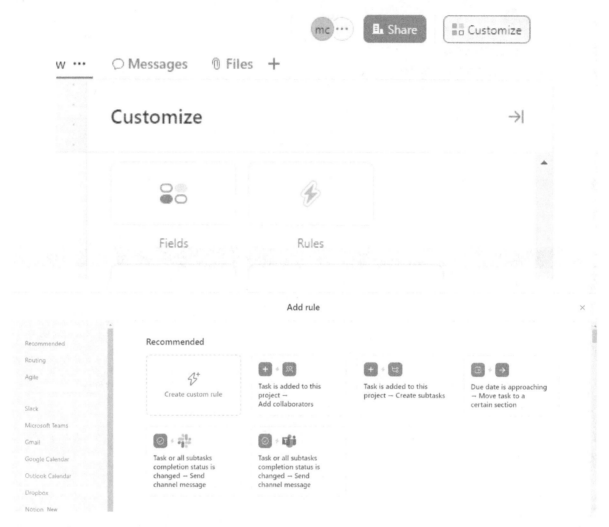

Rules are project-specific and trigger actions based on conditions like overdue tasks or changes in custom fields.

Each rule includes triggers and actions; triggers initiate rules, like task overdue, while actions execute tasks, such as adding comments as reminders. Rules activate upon creation but can be paused during adjustments.

A rule can feature multiple triggers or actions. For instance, in a creative requests project, changing a custom field indicating request stage can automatically move tasks to new sections, add collaborators, and create subtasks for approvals.

Rules can integrate external team tools into Asana workflows. You can also apply rules to My Tasks for efficient daily task management.

Reports and Analytics to Track Project Performance

Reports and analytics in Asana are essential tools for monitoring and improving project performance. Here's a guide on how to effectively utilize them:

Accessing Reports:

- Navigate to the side bar.

- Click on "Reporting."

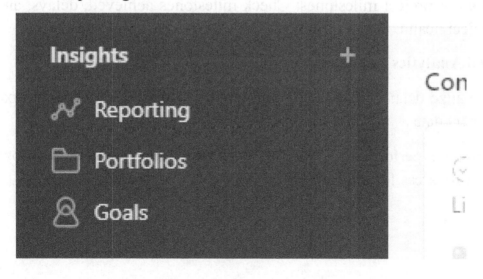

Generating Reports:

- Click on 'Create' to create a new report.

- Choose the type of report you need, such as task progress, workload, or project status.

- Customize the report parameters, including time frames, specific tasks, or team members to include.

Analysing Project Metrics:

- Track task progress: Monitor completion rates, overdue tasks, and upcoming deadlines.

- Assess workload distribution: Review how tasks are allocated among team members.

- Monitor project milestones: Check milestones achieved, delays, and overall project health.

Advanced Analytics Features:

- Visualize data: Utilize charts and graphs to visualize trends and patterns in project data.

- Compare performance: Analyse historical data to measure progress and identify areas for improvement.

Sharing and Utilizing Reports:

- Share reports with stakeholders: Communicate project status and performance metrics effectively.

- Inform decision-making: Use insights gained from reports to make informed decisions, adjust strategies, or reallocate resources.

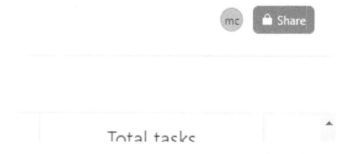

By leveraging Asana's reports and analytics, teams can effectively track project performance, improve productivity, and ensure project goals are achieved efficiently.

CHAPTER SEVEN
INTEGRATING ASANA WITH YOUR FAVORITE TOOLS

Streamlining Workflows with Third-Party Integrations

Asana excels at project management, but its true power lies in its ability to connect with your existing workflow. By leveraging third-party integrations, you can bridge the gap between Asana and your favourite tools, fostering seamless collaboration and boosting overall efficiency. Here's a guide to unlocking the potential of Asana integrations:

Identifying Integration Needs:

- Team Workflows: Analyse how your team currently works. Which tools do they use most frequently (email, communication platforms, file storage)?

- Project Requirements: Pinpoint specific project needs. Does your project require time tracking, design collaboration, or marketing automation tools?

Exploring Integration Options:

Asana offers a robust integration ecosystem with two primary methods for connecting with third-party tools:

- Built-in Integrations: Asana integrates natively with a vast array of popular tools. These integrations are readily available within Asana and require minimal setup.

- Zapier: Asana connects with hundreds of additional tools through Zapier, a third-party automation platform. Use Zapier for tools not directly supported by Asana.

Popular Integration Categories and Use Cases:

Communication & Collaboration:

- Integrate with Slack or Microsoft Teams to receive task notifications and updates within your preferred communication channels.

- Facilitate real-time discussions and brainstorming sessions directly within Asana tasks.

File Sharing & Storage:

- Connect with cloud storage services like Dropbox, Google Drive, or Box to attach files directly to Asana tasks, ensuring everyone has access to the latest versions.

- Eliminate the need for email attachments and version control struggles.

Email Management:

- Integrate with email clients like Gmail or Outlook to convert emails into actionable Asana tasks.

- Streamline project communication by centralizing tasks and discussions within Asana.

Calendar & Scheduling:

- Synchronize Asana tasks with your calendar (e.g., Google Calendar) to visualize deadlines and project timelines alongside other commitments.

- Ensure everyone on the team is aware of upcoming deadlines and task dependencies.

Time Tracking & Productivity:

- Integrate with time tracking tools like Harvest or Clockify to track time spent on tasks directly within Asana.

- Gain insights into project time allocation and identify areas for optimization.

- Enhance project budgeting and resource management with accurate time tracking data.

Benefits of Third-Party Integrations:

- Reduced Context Switching: Keep everything centralized and accessible within your preferred tools, eliminating the need to jump between applications.

- Enhanced Collaboration: Foster seamless communication and information sharing between team members and external collaborators.

- Automated Workflows: Eliminate repetitive tasks by setting up automated actions (e.g., automatically create tasks from emails, update calendars with deadlines).

- Improved Data Visibility: Gain a consolidated view of your project across different tools, ensuring everyone is on the same page.

Choosing the Right Integrations:

- Prioritize Core Needs: Focus on integrating the tools your team uses most frequently to streamline their daily workflows.

- Consider Ease of Use: Opt for integrations with user-friendly interfaces and simple setup processes to minimize disruption.

- Security Considerations: Ensure all integrated tools meet your organization's security standards. Research data privacy practices and access controls offered by each integration.

Taking Advantage of Advanced Features (Paid Plans):

- Asana's paid plans offer additional functionalities for integrations:

- Customizable Workflows: Create complex automation sequences using Zapier to connect multiple tools and automate intricate workflows.

- Advanced Data Mapping: Map data fields between Asana and other tools to ensure seamless information exchange and avoid manual data entry.

By strategically integrating Asana with third-party tools, you can break down communication barriers, automate repetitive tasks, and empower your team to work more efficiently. Remember, the right integrations can transform Asana from a project management tool into the central nervous system of your entire team's work.

Connecting Asana with Email, Calendar and Productivity Apps

Asana thrives on collaboration, and integrating it with your preferred tools enhances its capabilities. Here's a guide to streamline your workflow by connecting Asana with email, calendar, and productivity apps.

Connecting Asana with Email:

- Identify Your Email Provider: Choose from popular providers like Gmail, Outlook, etc.

- Locate Integrations: Click on the "Profile" icon at the top-right corner.

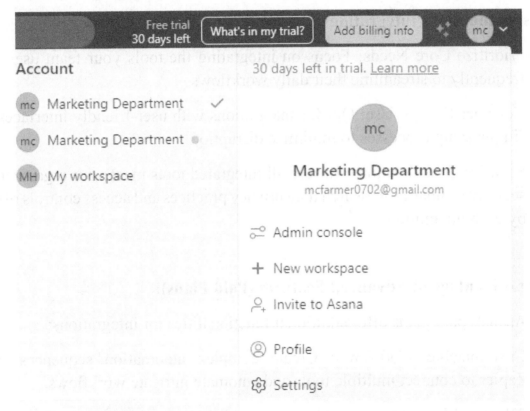

- Click on "Settings" and click on "Apps."

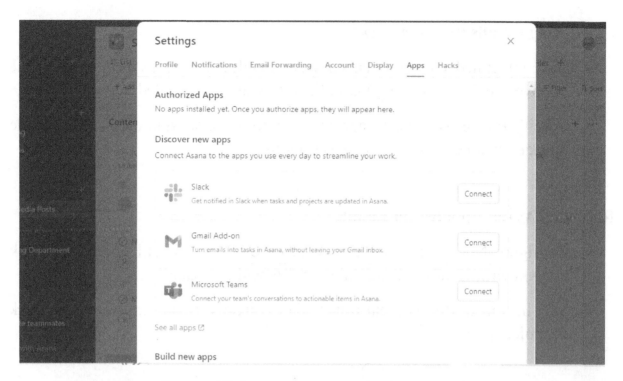

- Follow Setup Steps: Click on "Connect" in front of "Gmail Add-on. Asana guides you through an easy setup process, typically involving authorizing your account.

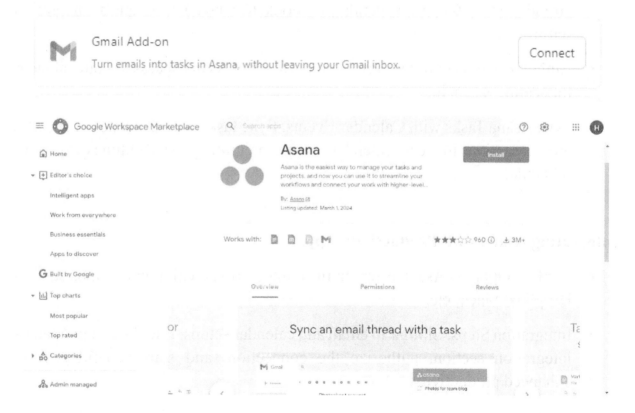

Converting Emails to Asana Tasks:

- Once integrated, convert emails into actionable Asana tasks using options like "Convert to Task" in your email client or Asana's dedicated button.

- Specify Project Details: Assign tasks to projects, set due dates, and include relevant email content in task descriptions.

Receiving Asana Updates via Email:

- Configure Notification Settings: Choose to receive email updates for task assignments, comments, and other events within Asana.

- Stay Informed: Receive real-time updates directly in your inbox to keep track of project progress.

Connecting Asana with Your Calendar:

- Find Calendar Integration: Similar to email setup, locate your calendar provider (e.g., Google Calendar, Outlook Calendar) in Asana's integration settings.

- Authorize Connection: Follow prompts to grant Asana access to your calendar for seamless syncing.

- Sync Asana Tasks with Calendar Events: Sync tasks with due dates or specific project sections to create calendar events, integrating task deadlines with your schedule.

Integrating Asana with Productivity Apps:

- Explore Options: Asana offers built-in integrations with popular apps such as Dropbox, Slack, etc.

- Integration Steps: Similar to email and calendar setups, find the app in Asana's integration section, authorize the connection, and start benefiting from enhanced productivity.

- Use Zapier for Custom Integrations: For apps not directly supported by Asana, leverage Zapier to create custom integrations tailored to your needs.

Additional Tips:

- Review Integration Options: Explore Asana's extensive integration library to find tools that best complement your workflow.

- Start with Core Integrations: Begin by connecting Asana with essential tools you use daily, like email and calendar.

Security Considerations: Before integrating any tool, ensure it aligns with your organization's security standards. Research data privacy practices and access controls provided by the integration.

CHAPTER EIGHT
CUSTOMIZING ASANA FOR YOUR NEEDS

Creating Custom Workflows and Dashboards

Creating customized workflows and dashboards within Asana can greatly enhance your project management capabilities. Here's a guide to help you effectively create them:

Creating Custom Workflows:

Define Workflow Stages:

- Identify and outline the stages or phases that tasks will move through in your project. Examples include stages like "To-Do," "In Progress," "Review," and "Completed."

Set Up Sections in Asana:

- Create distinct sections within your project to represent each workflow stage. These sections visually organize tasks and indicate their progress.

Utilize Custom Fields:

- Define specific custom fields in Asana to capture detailed information about tasks that align with your workflow requirements. These fields can include priority levels, status updates, task types, or other relevant metadata.

Establish Task Dependencies:

- Use task dependencies to link tasks in sequential order where one task must be completed before another can begin. This feature helps in visualizing and managing task dependencies effectively.

Automate Routine Actions:

- Take advantage of Asana's automation capabilities to automate repetitive tasks. Set up rules to automatically assign tasks, update task statuses, or send notifications based on predefined triggers such as task completion or approaching due dates.

Document Workflow Guidelines:

- Document the defined workflow stages, task dependencies, and automation rules within Asana. This documentation ensures clarity and consistency in how tasks progress through the workflow stages.

Creating Dashboards:

Identify Key Metrics and Goals:

- Determine the critical project metrics and goals that need tracking. Examples include task completion rates, project milestones, team workload distribution, and budget status.

Select Dashboard Widgets:

- Choose and configure dashboard widgets within Asana to display relevant metrics and information. Widgets can include task lists, charts, project status summaries, and more, tailored to your project's specific needs.

Customize Dashboard Views:

- Customize dashboard views by arranging widgets and organizing information to suit your preferences. You can create multiple dashboards as needed for different projects, teams, or specific metrics.

Monitor Real-Time Updates:

- Ensure that dashboard data updates in real-time to provide accurate insights into project performance. Real-time updates enable informed decision-making and timely adjustments as needed.

Share and Collaborate:

- Share dashboards with team members or stakeholders who require visibility into project progress. Set appropriate permissions to ensure data security and control access to sensitive information.

Review and Adjust:

- Regularly review dashboard metrics to track progress against set goals and identify areas for improvement. Adjust dashboard configurations based on evolving project requirements and feedback to optimize performance.

By following these steps to create custom workflows and dashboards in Asana, you can streamline project management processes, enhance team collaboration, and gain deeper insights into project performance. Tailoring workflows and dashboards to your project's specific needs promotes efficiency and contributes to achieving project success.

Using Asana Forms and Portfolios

Asana provides robust capabilities beyond basic task management. Here's a guide on how to leverage Asana Forms and Portfolios for enhanced project organization and efficient data collection:

Creating Asana Forms for Efficient Data Gathering:

- Access Point: Forms can be created within any Asana project. Navigate to the project's "Customize" menu and select "Forms" from the dropdown.

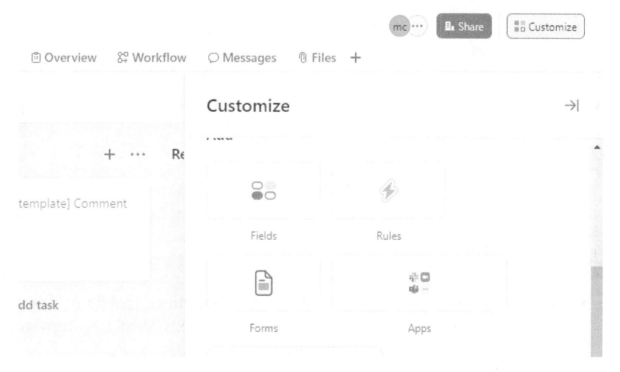

- Building Your Form: Use Asana's intuitive interface to drag-and-drop various question types (text, numbers, dates, drop-down lists) to construct your form.

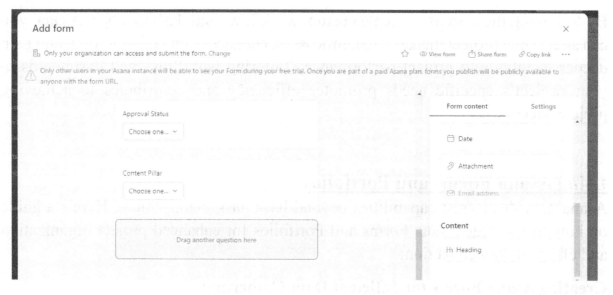

- Customizing the Form: Add a title, description, and logo to enhance clarity and branding.

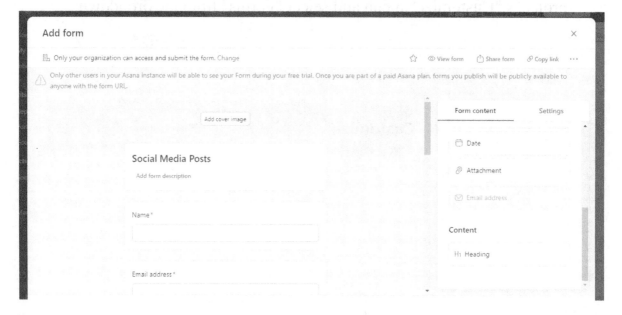

- Setting Up Submission Options: Define access settings (public or private within your company) and specify how submissions should be managed (create new tasks or update existing ones).

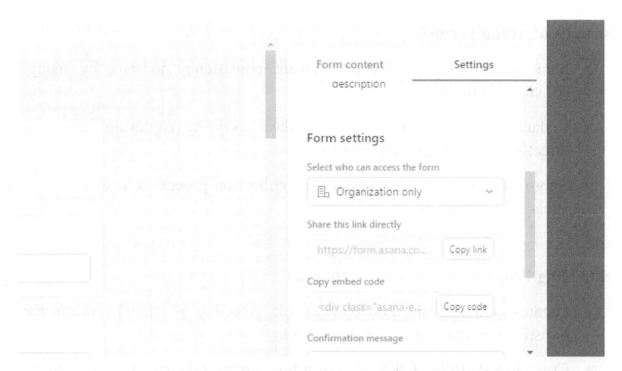

- **Publishing and Sharing:** Once finalized, publish the form and share the link with intended respondents.

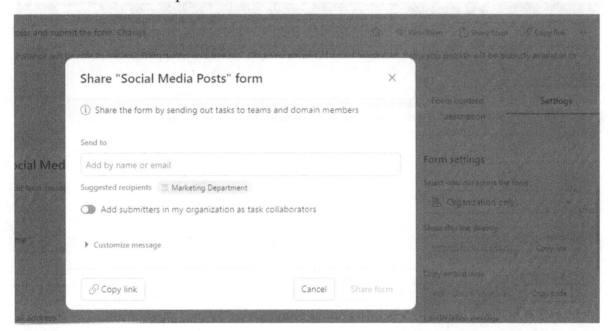

Benefits of Asana Forms:

- Standardized Data Collection: Ensure consistency in data by using a structured form format.

- Reduced Manual Work: Automate data entry by capturing information directly through form submissions.

- Improved Efficiency: Streamline data collection processes to save time and enhance productivity.

Managing Projects with Asana Portfolios:

- Organization at Scale: Portfolios enable grouping of related projects for a holistic view and strategic management.

- Creating a Portfolio: Click on "Portfolios" on the side bar, click "Create, then add your preferred name and choose other options to continue."

- Click on "Got to Portfolio" and navigate to select the projects and portfolios to add.

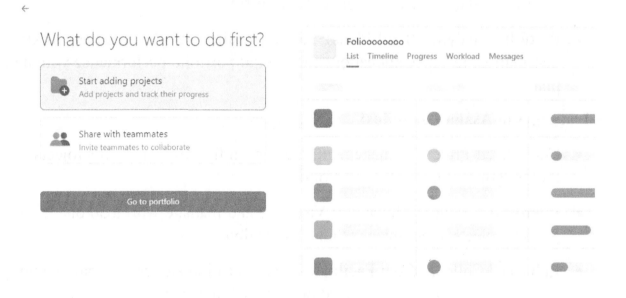

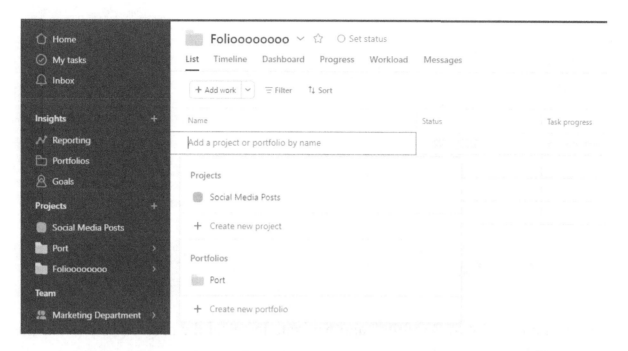

- Portfolio Views: Choose from list or kanban board views to visualize project progress and dependencies across your portfolio.

- Portfolio Analytics (Paid Plans): Access detailed insights such as workload distribution, resource allocation, and overall portfolio performance with paid plans.

Advantages of Asana Portfolios:

- Centralized Project Management: Gain a unified overview of projects and their relationships within a portfolio.

- Improved Resource Allocation: Visualize and manage workload distribution across projects to optimize resource allocation.

- Enhanced Collaboration: Facilitate communication and collaboration among teams working on interconnected projects within a portfolio.

Integrating Forms with Portfolios:

- Use Asana Forms in conjunction with Portfolios to streamline data collection across multiple projects:

- Create a form tailored to collect relevant data for portfolio projects.

- Share the form link for data submission.

- Configure portfolio settings to automate task creation or updates based on form submissions.

Additional Tips:

- Integrate Forms with Workflows: Automate actions triggered by form submissions, such as task assignment based on submitted data.

- Customize Portfolio Views: Tailor portfolio views to highlight critical information like deadlines, task completion rates, or resource utilization.

Advanced Features for Power Users

Asana provides a comprehensive feature set that meets the needs of both novice users and advanced project management professionals. Here's an overview of advanced functionalities that can maximize Asana's capabilities for power users:

Custom Workflows and Automation:

- Advanced Automation: Beyond basic rules, power users can create intricate workflows with multiple triggers, conditions, and actions in Asana. This capability allows for highly tailored automation sequences that streamline complex processes.

- Zapier Integration: Integrate Asana with a wide range of tools via Zapier, enabling complex multi-step workflows and expanding automation possibilities beyond Asana's native features.

Advanced Analytics (Paid Plans):

- Burn Down Charts and Resource Management: Paid plans offer tools like burn down charts to visualize task completion rates over time, aiding in identifying bottlenecks and optimizing resource allocation.

- Team Efficiency Analysis: Analyse team and individual productivity metrics to pinpoint areas for improvement and optimize workflows, facilitating data-driven decisions about resource management.

Portfolios and Custom Fields:

- Portfolio Reporting: With paid plans, generate comprehensive reports at the portfolio level to monitor project performance across multiple projects. This feature allows power users to track progress, spot trends, and make strategic decisions based on portfolio-wide data.

- Custom Fields: Create tailored custom fields (e.g., text, numbers, dates, dropdowns) to capture detailed project information beyond basic task details. Custom fields enable advanced filtering, reporting, and data analysis tailored to specific project needs.

Advanced Search and Reporting:

- Enhanced Search Functionality: Asana offers powerful search capabilities with advanced operators and filters, enabling precise retrieval of tasks and data points. This capability supports efficient information retrieval and facilitates informed decision-making.

- Customizable Reports (Paid Plans): Paid plans provide the flexibility to create custom reports with specific data points and visualizations tailored to project requirements. Power users can leverage this feature to generate insightful reports for stakeholders.

Asana API:

- API Integration: Asana's API allows developers and technically proficient users to integrate Asana with custom applications or build additional functionalities on top of Asana's core features. This capability offers extensive customization and automation opportunities.

Additional Tips:

- Explore Third-Party Integrations: Asana's Marketplace offers a wide array of integrations that can further extend Asana's functionality, catering to specific needs of power users.

- Stay Informed: Keep abreast of Asana's updates and new features to leverage the latest capabilities for optimizing project management workflows.

Asana Certification: Consider pursuing Asana certification to deepen your understanding and proficiency in utilizing its advanced features effectively.

CHAPTER NINE
ASANA TIPS AND BEST PRACTICES
Effective Task Management Strategies

Implementing effective task management strategies in Asana can significantly boost productivity and project success. Here's how to utilize Asana's features for streamlined task management:

Task Organization and Prioritization:

- Organize tasks into sections within projects to categorize them by stages or priority levels (e.g., To-Do, In Progress, Completed).

- Utilize custom fields or tags in Asana to mark tasks by priority (e.g., High, Medium, Low) for easy identification.

Clear Task Details and Assignments:

- Ensure each task includes clear descriptions outlining objectives, requirements, and relevant details.

- Assign tasks to specific team members within Asana to define responsibilities and ensure accountability.

Deadline Management:

- Set realistic due dates for tasks to maintain project timelines. Asana allows for assigning due dates and sending reminders to team members.

- Utilize task dependencies in Asana to sequence tasks logically, ensuring they are completed in the correct order.

Collaborative Tools and Communication:

- Use task comments in Asana to facilitate collaboration, provide updates, ask questions, and discuss task-related matters.

- Directly notify team members using @mentions in comments to engage them in discussions or seek input.

Automation and Efficiency:

- Leverage automation rules in Asana to automate repetitive tasks, such as assigning tasks based on triggers or updating task statuses automatically.

- Create task templates in Asana for recurring tasks or processes to save time and maintain consistency across projects.

Progress Tracking and Reporting:

- Utilize Asana's dashboard feature to monitor project progress, track task completion rates, and visualize key metrics.

- Generate reports in Asana to analyse team performance, identify bottlenecks, and make data-driven decisions for project improvements.

Integration with External Tools:

- Connect Asana with email to convert emails into actionable tasks directly within Asana, centralizing all communications.

- Sync Asana tasks with calendar apps for effective management of deadlines and milestones.

By implementing these task management strategies in Asana, teams can enhance collaboration, streamline workflows, and achieve higher efficiency in project execution.

Maintaining Project Focus

Maintaining project focus and avoiding common issues are essential for successful project management. Here's a guide on how to achieve this in Asana:

Clear Project Scope and Objectives:

- Define clear project goals, scope, and deliverables from the outset.

- Use Asana to document and communicate project objectives in the project overview or description.

Effective Planning and Scheduling:

- Break down the project into manageable tasks and subtasks using Asana's features.

- Assign due dates and priorities to tasks to create a timeline and keep deadlines in focus.

Regular Progress Tracking:

- Use Asana's progress dashboard to monitor task completion rates, milestones, and overall project progress.

- Regularly update task statuses to accurately reflect progress and identify potential delays early.

Communication and Collaboration:

- Foster open communication among team members using Asana's comments and @mentions.

- Use task comments to discuss updates, clarify requirements, and address issues promptly.

Managing Changes Effectively:

- Implement change management protocols in Asana to handle scope changes or new requirements.

- Use task dependencies and timeline adjustments to manage changes without losing focus on the project.

Risk Management:

- Identify potential risks early in the project and document them using Asana's task notes or custom fields.

- Assign team members to monitor and mitigate risks throughout the project lifecycle.

Regular Review and Evaluation:

- Schedule regular project review meetings or checkpoints using Asana tasks or calendar integration.

- Evaluate project progress against initial goals and adjust strategies as needed to maintain focus.

Avoiding Common Issues:

- Avoid scope creep by clearly defining project boundaries and managing change requests effectively.

Address communication gaps quickly to prevent misunderstandings or delays in task execution.

CHAPTER TEN
ASANA HELP AND SUPPORT RESOURCES

Keyboard Shortcuts

Here's a breakdown of essential Asana keyboard shortcuts to navigate the platform like a pro:

Navigation:

- Tab + Z: Go to My Tasks.

- Tab + I: Go to Inbox.

- Tab + O: Hide/unhide Sidebar.

- Tab + .: Create a new Section (in a project).

- Tab + P: Add your task to a project.

- Tab + N: Create a new task (above the current task).

- ↑/↓: Move up/down through tasks.

- Tab + Backspace: Remove selected task(s).

- Esc: Collapse the right pane.

Task Actions:

- Enter: Create a new task (below the current task).

- Tab + Enter: Mark a task as Complete.

- Tab + C: Add a comment to the selected task.

- Tab + A: Assign the selected task to someone.

- Tab + D: Assign a due date to the selected task.

- Tab + F: Add a Follower to the selected task.

- Tab + T: Assign a tag to the selected task.

- Tab + S: Focus on Subtasks.

- Tab + X: Full-screen task.

Selection:

- ↑/↓: Change selection (up/down).
- Shift-Click: Select range of tasks.

Application:

- ⌘/ or Ctrl/: Show keyboard shortcuts (⌘ for Mac, Ctrl for Windows).

Practice makes perfect: Spend some time familiarizing yourself with the most frequently used shortcuts to improve your Asana workflow.

Support Resources

Asana offers a variety of resources to help users maximize their experience on the platform, regardless of their skill level. Here's an overview of the key support resources available:

Asana Help Centre:

Primary Resource: The Asana Help Centre is your go-to destination for all Asana support needs, providing a comprehensive collection of articles, tutorials, and guides on various topics:

- Getting started with Asana
- Managing tasks, projects, and portfolios
- Using features like automation, forms, and reporting
- Troubleshooting common issues

Search Functionality: Use the Help Centre's powerful search function by entering your question or keyword to find relevant articles and resources.

- https://help.asana.com/hc/en-us

Asana Academy:

In-Depth Learning: Asana Academy offers self-paced online courses to help you master Asana's functionalities, covering topics from basic project management principles to advanced features.

Free and Paid Courses: Asana Academy provides both free and paid courses. Free courses offer a solid foundation, while paid courses delve deeper into specific topics.

- https://academy.asana.com/

Asana Community Forum:

Community Connection: The Asana Community Forum is a vibrant platform where you can connect with other users, ask questions, share tips and tricks, and get help from experts.

Search Discussions: Before posting a new question, check if it has already been addressed by searching existing discussions.

- https://forum.asana.com/c/forum-en/160

Asana Support (Paid Plans):

Dedicated Support: Users on paid Asana plans have access to dedicated support options, which may include email or phone support, depending on the plan level.

Subscription Requirement: Dedicated support is typically available only for paid plan users.

Additional Resources:

Asana YouTube Channel: Access helpful video tutorials and demonstrations of various Asana features on their YouTube channel.

Asana Blog: Stay updated on the latest Asana developments, product announcements, and project management best practices by following the Asana blog.

- https://m.youtube.com/watch?v=uCDftAtr9tI
- https://blog.asana.com/

The Asana community is extensive and continually growing, so don't hesitate to reach out and benefit from the collective knowledge and experience of other Asana enthusiast.

CHAPTER ELEVEN
APPENDIX

Asana Glossary of Terms

Tasks: The fundamental units of work in Asana, representing individual actions or deliverables. You can assign them to team members, set deadlines, prioritize them, and attach relevant files.

Projects: Collections of tasks grouped together to achieve a specific goal. Projects can be organized in different views (list or board) to manage larger initiatives.

Workspaces: Shared spaces for collaboration, where teams work on related projects and tasks. Ideal for small teams or individuals.

Organizations: Larger entities within Asana, typically representing companies or large teams. They contain multiple workspaces and teams, facilitating broader collaboration.

Teams: Subsets of an organization, grouping people who collaborate on related projects. Teams can have multiple projects and are used to organize work by department or function.

Sections: A way to categorize tasks within a project, often representing stages or categories. Sections help break down projects and improve task visibility.

Subtasks: Tasks nested under another task, used to further break down larger tasks into smaller, more manageable steps.

Milestones: Special tasks representing significant achievements or key points in a project timeline. Milestones help visualize major progress markers.

Dependencies: Relationships between tasks, where one task must be completed before another can begin. Dependencies ensure proper workflow order.

Custom Fields: User-defined fields added to tasks or projects to capture specific data relevant to your project needs. These can be text, numbers, dates, or dropdown options.

Timeline: A visual representation of a project's schedule, showing tasks, their durations, and dependencies. Timelines help plan projects and track progress over time.

Dashboards: Customizable overviews of project metrics and progress using different widgets. Dashboards provide insights into project status, team workload, and other key performance indicators (KPIs).

Portfolios: Collections of related projects grouped together for high-level tracking and management. Portfolios offer a consolidated view of progress across multiple projects.

Goals: High-level objectives aligned with the organization's strategic aims. Goals help track progress toward larger outcomes and can be linked to specific projects or tasks.

Comments: Notes or feedback left on a task for communication and collaboration. Comments help team members discuss tasks, provide updates, and share information.

Inbox: A central location for notifications about task updates, comments, and mentions. The inbox keeps users informed about project changes and communications.

Tags: Labels added to tasks for easier search and filtering by themes, priorities, or other criteria not covered by sections or projects.

Attachments: Files or documents linked to a task for reference or collaboration. Attachments provide relevant resources directly within tasks.

Forms: Customizable forms used to collect structured information from team members or external stakeholders. Form submissions create tasks, streamlining data collection and task creation.

Templates: Pre-designed project or task structures that can be reused to maintain consistency and save time. Templates help standardize workflows across similar projects or tasks.

Workload: A feature that provides a visual overview of each team member's assigned tasks, helping balance assignments and manage team capacity.

Rules: Automation features that trigger specific actions based on predefined conditions. Rules automate repetitive tasks, such as assigning tasks or updating statuses.

Project Overview: A central hub within a project that provides high-level information and context, including the project brief, key milestones, and status updates.

Advanced Search: A powerful tool that allows users to find tasks, projects, or conversations based on multiple criteria, enabling them to locate information quickly and efficiently.

Understanding and utilizing these terms, will help users navigate Asana more effectively and take full advantage of its capabilities to manage projects and tasks.

113

THANK YOU
FOR READING

Made in the USA
Middletown, DE
03 September 2024